OF SHADOW & LIGHT

By TMC Poetry

Of Shadow and Light

Copyright © 2022 by TMC Poetry

Author/Publisher

All rights reserved. This book or any portion thereof may not be reproduced or used in any manner whatsoever without the express written permission of the author/publisher, except for the use of brief quotations in a book review.

Printed in the United States of America

First Printing, 2022

All writings within this book belong to the author. Cover art, photography and design by TMC Poetry Author/Publisher/Professional Photographer

Of Shadow and Light

This book was written to give hope to those seeking light in the shadows of life's struggles and grievances. You are never alone in your battles. Thank you for being a constant support to me, my work and my family. I wouldn't be doing this if it weren't for your constant love. I send that same love and prayers of peace right back into the universe to you.

Of Shadow and Light

*To give light to them that sit in darkness
and in the shadow of death.
To guide our feet in the way
of peace.*

Luke 1:79

Of Shadow and Light

POEMS & PAGES

14. Savor

15. Enough

16. September

17. Karma

18. Splinters

20. Gripped

22. Beautiful Disaster

23. Words and Wine

24. Purgatory

25. Rabbit Hole

27. Little Girl

29. Daydream

31. Lucid

32. A Day in The Life

34. Somewhere That I Belong

36. Bury my Bones

37. Reject in The Attic

38. Legacy

39. The Jester

41. The Noose

42. Sanctuary

Of Shadow and Light

43. Crepuscule

44. The Veil

46. Happily, Ever After

48. On the Business of Writing

49. Draw Me A Line

50. Headfirst

51. A Warm and Welcoming Spring

52. Dignity

54. Masterpiece

55. You Are the Ocean

56. Muscle Memory

57. To Be Free

59. Freshly Pressed

60. Minced Words

61. The Constant Fault

62. Love Language

64. Dear Heart

65. Vulnerability

66. Deeply Woven

67. Broken Wings

68. Adonis

69. Jagged

Of Shadow and Light

70. I Miss You

72. Ruined

73. 2 AM

74. 3 AM Silence

76. Soul Partner

77. When You Weren't Looking

79. Grief

83. Trauma

84. Pressure

86. Nostalgia

88. Deception

89. Dare to Venture

90. Not in Love

91. A Letter to My Formal Self

93. Kaleidoscope

94. Consequential Love

96. Autumnal Grief

97. Hourglass Love

98. Lonely Souls

99. The Void

100. Bled

101. Conceal

Of Shadow and Light

102. Sliced Open
103. Bitter
104. Rainy Day Playlist
105. Eternal Balance
106. Twenty-Eight Stitches
108. Misplaced Fortunes
110. Sometimes
112. Beyond Measure
113. Absolution
114. Carnal Desires
116. Storm
117. Lighter Fluid
118. Sweater
120. Dove
122. Genius of Art
124. Mirage
125. Waves
127. Your Name
129. My Murderer
130. Destroy Me
131. Lock and Key
132. Shell

Of Shadow and Light

133. Lighthouse
134. Confessors
135. Dwell
137. Beckoning
139. Filter
141. Vibrancy
142. Absolution
143. Mirror
144. Sunsets
145. Moment's Notice
146. The New
148. Pepper Thin Skin
149. Home
150. Reasons
151. Death
153. Spectacle
154. Wash, Rinse and Repeat
155. The Taste of Love
157. Starter Fluid
158. Love Should Never Be
159. Lemonade
160. Shoreline

Of Shadow and Light

MICROS

163. Belonging

164. Recognize

165. Meaning

166. Drug

167. Within My Dreams

168. Madness

169. Courage

170. Soul

171. My Heart

172. Cruel

173. Tangled

174. Forged

175. Tragedy

176. Mountain

177. Tripping

179. Moonlight

178. Wounds

180. Bitterness Wept

181. In Helping You

182. Sun and Moon

Of Shadow and Light

183. Beautiful Way
184. Laced Deceit
185. Character
186. Life Preserver
187. Artificial Sweetener
188. Acceptance
189. Tragically
190. Giver
191. Truth
192. Answers
193. Stuff of Stars
194. Yours
195. Sanguine Veil
196. Tip of Your Tongue
197. Cuts Deeply
198. Loved by a Poet
199. Control
200. Power
201. Explain
202. Heal
203. Whole
204. New Year

Of Shadow and Light

205. Hard
206. Expands
207. Spell
208. Poetry
209. Aim
210. Deaf Ears
211. Seeps
212. Quietly
213. Hell
214. The Fire
215. Crumble
216. Buy
217. In My Silence
218. Monotony
219. Heard
220. I Am Not the Moon
221. The Light
222. Acceptance
223. Mask
224. Webs
225. Taste
226. Her Heart

Of Shadow and Light

227. Worth

228. Ravish

229. Unrealized Dream

230. Astray

231. Embers

232. Dwindles

233. Conundrum

234. Learning

235. Stumble

236. Unlearn

237. Ache

238. Junkie

239. You Don't Love Me

240. True

241. Convey

242. Chasing

243. How Many Lies

244. Memory

245. You and Me

246. Unwrap

247. Option

248. Excuses

Of Shadow and Light

249. Drowning
250. Outline
251. Silence
252. As I Am
253. Absence
254. Kingdom

Of Shadow and Light
Savor

I take your words into my mouth

I savor every drop of what you

Have fed me

You are smooth like silk

You soak into the skin with nourishment

That I have yearned for

And now your name rolls off the tongue

Deliciously as though it were meant to be

Of Shadow and Light
Enough

If only sorry were enough

Then maybe your shattered promises

Would've made a difference

Now we have regrets etched in black

Too late to pick apart

Those lips on my thighs

That tongue on my breasts

Not even such stolen moments could

Soothe the mess that we have made

I will let them burn with January's embers

So just kiss me quickly one last time

Before I leave you in the dark

Where you belong

Of Shadow and Light

September

It was always by September's end
When the soul left from my body
Or maybe it was my heart that
You always managed to rip from
My chest maybe you smelled the change
In chlorophyll draining the leaves
Of the color
Whatever the reason
Autumn became harder than
Winters freeze ever could
On my body

Of Shadow and Light

Karma

I kept you for as long as the breath

In my lungs allowed

The space between has grown so wide

And ocean has filled the void

Once the outsider

You became the flame that I saw

When I looked into the mirror

And how you burned

I became the ashes at your feet

Karma made a lap around

Yet I am the one paying for its lesson

And you – you're nowhere to be found

I mourn a ghost

A spirit of what I felt when you were

Still keeping me warm

Of Shadow and Light

Splinters

There is no love affair

held within these hands

I am reminded of this time and again

I own a one-sided splintered affection

For another soul who couldn't reciprocate

My intentions

And this seems to be the story that I read

One forlorn word at a time

To help my naïve little soul to sleep at night

This has become the middle of the night's truth

There is no moon

Nor stars in this childlike heart of mine

That could send me adrift counting sheep

But my ears and heart hold onto

The sound of his voice

Begging to slumber

Or better yet

A long-sought hibernation

Of Shadow and Light

My soul prays for release

Of Shadow and Light

Gripped

Gripped

Because there is no better way

To describe that I am frozen in fear

I am weighed down in a bottomless

Pit without any hope of returning

I am still

Quiet and unable to speak

Though my thoughts are spinning

At a gale like force

While a river of ice floods my chest

And rushes throughout

My circulatory system

This must be death

Or am I trapped in a nightmare

If this is my time to go

Take me home to ground zero

It might be my last chance at surviving

To remind me what a second lease

Of Shadow and Light

On life could look like
That I was once human
And maybe therein lies
The possibility of escaping this hell

Of Shadow and Light

Beautiful Disaster

There will always be that look
That catches my breath
A teleport into times past
A note that hits just the right chord
How no other love will ever touch me
As deeply as the one you carried
And still, I resent you
For what you have left me with
Because nothing else can compare
To what was shared between
Me and my lover
No other place will I ever be able
To call home like the space we created
In each other's hearts
In you
And only you
I blissfully and willingly come apart

Of Shadow and Light

Words & Wine

Words wrapped in wine

Flowed easier and tasted sweeter

Then those spoken off guard

But the iron thread has been severed

By suffocating repercussions

And I never seem to learn the lessons

That shouldn't be spoken

X marked the spot

Or maybe it's a bullseye that I can't

See placed over my heart

Continuously being shot with poisonous arrows

Nonetheless

My eager ears and eyes pray for an answer

But the chances are adding up

To the fact that time is passing through

An hourglass that cannot be retrieved

No matter how many times

I flip the damn thing back over

Of Shadow and Light

Purgatory

Maybe I shouldn't have built the wall
So high or expected cupid's arrow
To be drawn again
I gave up so many secrets and expected
Angels to descend from the heavens
With praise for all that I had confessed
Instead, I suffered the blow of curses
That hung over my head without
Knowing that I was paying the price
Of my ancestor's sins
And now there is nothing I can do
But wade through generational curses
As I wait for time to die
For the ghosts to come and keep me
Company or pray for your return
To revive my soul
From this purgatory

Of Shadow and Light

Rabbit Hole

She has broken bones set back in
The wrong places and her stiches
Get caught on anything she tries to
Quietly sneak by without
Causing any attention
Because she's had enough of the
Wrong sort
And that's what got her into
This mess in the first place
She longs for peace
In a world full of so much confusion
That she is often left not knowing
Which way is up
And which way is down
Though she desperately needs to know
Before she once again
Gets sucked right down into
The rabbit hole where all is lost

Of Shadow and Light

And rarely ever found again

Of Shadow and Light

Little Girl

Surviving off stories

And daydreams never seemed

To hurt anyone

Until I grew up and became

This codependent shell

That is supposedly a grown woman

I steal freedom from myself

And pass it along to someone else

Who is stronger and more capable

Of handling it than I am

I can't be trusted

Or left to my own devices

I can't make decisions without

Second guessing

And then, guessing again and again

Often seeking another's validation

Sure, she looks good on paper

But try throwing her to the wolves

Of Shadow and Light

And see how she fairs under

Red skies and watchful eyes

Let's see how far she can make it

Before panic sets in and she is crumbled

Up in a weary ball of fear

Peel back the skin

One naïve and misguided

Layer at a time and a shaken

Little girl is what you'll reveal

Of Shadow and Light

Daydream

We sip our morning coffees

Over gloomy skies and a

Brick hearth

You gently caress my open wrist

And brush the hair from

My eye and brow

And a soothing electricity transfers

From you into me

And now I have forgotten what was

Just at the tip of my tongue

You have such a beautiful way

Of distracting my thoughts

And I am taken back to last nights

Moments of indulgence when your

Hand cupped my face

Our eyes lock in adoration

Deep breath in

And back out again

Of Shadow and Light

Like a spell we are casting
Between us
And there is no other heart
I can imagine belonging to
Other than your own

Of Shadow and Light

Lucid

Time crashes into me

Quicker than my lungs take in air

And never as gracefully as the

Crow extends its delicate wings

I shed my skin to take on

Happier things

But there is a chill to the air

Gripping my heart

Rendering its beats

And causing it to seize

I must douse myself in

Formaldehyde to keep

The emotions fresh longer

Or the prickly heat will devour me

Tell me where I went wrong

So that I might wake from

This lucid dream

Of Shadow and Light

A Day in The Life

Let's talk about what it's like
To be me for a moment
Maybe it'll help you understand
Why I am up and down on any
Given day
And never expect the same person
From your yesterday
There's a good chance she won't be
Returning for a short while
Waking up is sometimes
A nightmare with a stark reminder
That life will never be the same
Before that diagnosis
You now that fresh optimism that
Swirls in your belly sometimes
How a new day is always on the horizon
That is gone for me
Along with the hopes of the man he

Of Shadow and Light

Was meant to be and dreamed up

From my childhood fantasies

When I would grow up to someday

Become a mother

Instead, my thoughts drift to wheelchairs

And our homes capabilities

To accommodate them

Or what will the day be like when I

Must kiss my boy good-bye for

The last time

Or watch as they close the casket

On his little face

The face that looks so much like

My daddy

This anticipatory grief is a thief

And my heart and mind become

A chore when all I wanted

Were the things that I finally

Did receive but with such

Heavy and unbearable conditions

Of Shadow and Light

Somewhere That I Belong

I belong with the downtrodden

And the broken hearted

The addicts and the trauma survivors

The rejects and the lovers

With nothing better to do

Than to drink the night away

I belong in all black

With my guitar as an accessory

In smoky dive bars and nightclubs

Up against sweaty bodies

Body surfing to music loud enough

To blow my ear drums out

Where there are phone numbers and obscenities

Cover bathroom stalls and there's

A girl puking her guts out in one over

But when I walk back out

It's all good cause the dude across the way

Who was eyeing me earlier that night

Looks like something out of

Of Shadow and Light

One of my favorite music videos
And maybe this was the night
That I get lucky with forever
Because I am finally somewhere
That I belong

Of Shadow and Light

Bury My Bones

How do I thrive

Clipped and broken

Do I wait for the seed to

Take root and grow

Should I ring out the rain

When there are so few clouds

That linger

I am so far from a place to

Call my own

How did I go wrong to feel

Such a betrayal

By the vines that bear little fruit

That I have tenderly cared for

Do I give up the ghost and take

Refuge in the soil

Is this the final resting place

I'm meant to bury my bones

Of Shadow and Light

Reject In the Attic

Such a beautiful face

But you don't speak my language

Have I come this far

To give up the dream I have been

Nursing since I was a small girl

A promise I made to myself

But everyone else has me

Seeing in jade with their

Destined love affairs

Always falling for the puzzle

Piece that I never quite fit with

I'm another reject in the attic

The flower standing against the wall

A back up plan

But never the trophy

Placed upon the mantle

Of Shadow and Light

Legacy

I will leave behind a legacy

Of misunderstandings

I've built a small world

That no one else can seem

To fit into

Maybe it's all been circumstance

That my life has been this way

Or maybe it is I who is

At fault for the loneliness

That creeps in and settles

It is heaviness cannot be ignored

The hope never seems to last

And I can feel it

As I run out of doors

That close shut behind me

There is no outrunning

These ghosts that gain on me

Of Shadow and Light

The Jester

I have given away so many pieces of me

That I can't recognize

The woman I drew myself out

To be anymore

Because you see

I planned out love like a fairytale

A concoction of all the right

Words, themes and love songs

The right moments and mannerisms

With just the right verses to strum

It all along

But the more that I evolve I can

See my fictitious world and how it

All plays out

Frogs never become princes

As I am not the princess

But in truth, the court jester

Only here for everyone else's

Of Shadow and Light

Entertainment

Of Shadow and Light

The Noose

Why am I here when

I could remain in such a dark place

But each precious face keeps me grounded

Tethered to this mortal realm

When I think about the cold floor

Curling into a ball

Holding my breath

Letting it out again

Or choking my own neck

Letting the noose dangle in

Front of my face

But no

I choose to move forward

Because theirs is the love that

Keeps me tethered to this life

Until the inevitable end

I only wish accepting my truth

Wasn't quite so hard to swallow

Of Shadow and Light

Sanctuary

I bear the weight of truth
On crumbled shoulders
I've dug a hole
To bury my dreams
Six feet under
With calloused hands
And an afflicted heart
I bear witness to fortunes past
A ticking clock
Softly begging me but
I settle for sanctuary instead

Of Shadow and Light

Crepuscule

I crawl in bleak

Vastness

I starve for truth

And grasp for light

In the darkness

With little hope of a

Subtle glow

The familiarity of

The crepuscule

A humid blanket

To keep me soothed

And distracted

At a standstill

Though I can't seem to

Recall where it was that

I am meant to be

Of Shadow and Light

The Veil

Do we overlook the significance
And the great vastness of the cosmos
Its boundless infinity
Versus our infinite minds
How are we meant to grab ahold
Of the dimensional veils to
Rip them down
Catching a glimpse of doorways
That reach in oblivion
And the greatest secrets
To the constants of our wandering
Souls and their longing
We are meant to live
In five-dimensional magnificence
Expanding our existences
Finally living how we were
Meant to be
That death is not the end

Of Shadow and Light

It is always a beginning

Of Shadow and Light

Happily, Ever After

Loneliness kicks in like clockwork

First thing in the morning

That's when I wind myself up

Slap the mask on

And quietly rev the engine

And if sleep didn't grant me rest

The night before

I give myself a little more gas

To get by

And it's exhausting

Keeping the ship afloat

Staying clear of the rocks

Having to always think before acting

Before opening my mouth

And allowing my mind its freedom

Having to put other's needs

Before my own

My swollen heart pays for

Of Shadow and Light

Its crimes in so many ways

I am petrified by the end

Of each day

If this is truly my happily ever after

Or did I let it slip away

Of Shadow and Light

On The Business of Writing

What if I ran out of words

And have nothing left to give

Do I cut myself and bleed

Should I force love again

Because the hungry need

Their fulfillment

When empty stomachs

Lurch and growl

Or would anyone even

Take notice

That I was no

Longer around

Of Shadow and Light

Draw Me A Line

The alcohol has long

Dried out but I need

Another glass of whatever

You've got flowing

Life has perched itself

On my shoulders

For far too long now

And I am dying for a trip

Somewhere into oblivion

But I'll need another

Ticket back to reality

When it's all said and done

Though I wish I didn't need it

Because my time on this

Planet is short

So for the sake of living a little

Pour me another drink

And draw me another line

Of Shadow and Light

Headfirst

I am a free-flowing current
Desperately reaching your shore
The hand that searches
For true meaning
Then at long last
Finding yours
The crisp first
Sip of water
To finally quench your thirst
And if I could be
Your ever after
I would come running
Headfirst

Of Shadow and Light

A Warm and Welcoming Spring

Oh, how the whirling of the wind

Frames my broken

Fragile heart

Though it's frigid icy breath

Has yet to make it stop

So, for now I will lie still

For now, I will brave

The elements

Knowing that even the most

Brutal of winters

Birth the dawn of a

Warm and welcoming spring

Of Shadow and Light

Dignity

But you liked it
Didn't you
The way that I moved
Above you
You licked every last
Thrust of my dignity
Only to feed the cause
Of your insatiable ego
And I fell for it
I believed I was the center
Of your affections
Though only ever the flow
Of your fickle heart
I should've given you just
A taste
A temptation of the
Delicacies that I embody
Instead, I handed out
Mouthfuls enough to spoil

Of Shadow and Light

Even my own appetite

Of Shadow and Light

Masterpiece

You perform a masterpiece

Of such distortion

A cacophonous audio matrix

And then call it love

I was never your medicine

Though you were my poison

And I am desperate to bleed you

From my system

You are the source of my

Deepest grievances

And you enjoy dancing

With your demons

Thought I should be

Grateful that you are now gone

I'm still contemplating

All the reasons

Of Shadow and Light

You Are the Ocean

Love comes in waves

And you are the ocean

I dive in deep

And I do not lose air

You purify my soul

You are the salt of the earth

I yield to your current

As you carry me to your shore

Of Shadow and Light

Muscle Memory

Lie next to me
I need to listen to
Your heart beating
A rhythmic lullaby that
Sings me fast asleep
I am learning your taste
You fill my lungs
Breathing you in deeply
As you become my heart's
Muscle memory

Of Shadow and Light

To Be Free

To be free

Doesn't mean the wind

Blowing in my hair

It's having the courage to

Allow the voice that lives

Tucked away and deep down

Where no one goes

It's opening my mouth

Without the worry of judgement

And sitting outside on an autumnal

Afternoon with a good book in hand

I take showers without asking

For permission and jump

Into the car without aim

Though freedom is in the eye

Of the beholder

There is no war knocking

On my front door or worry

Of food rations and empty bellies

Of Shadow and Light

Just keep the balance my

Mind tells me

For it could always be far worse

Then the hand that

Life has dealt me

Of Shadow and Light

Freshly Pressed

I am no longer crisp

Like freshly pressed linens

There is a staleness to me

That has reluctantly set in

One last babe rests at my bosom

I pushed the boundaries

And life humored me one last time

I collect my reflections at

Each days ending

As I count my many blessings

How did these moments get

So far away from me

My childlike optimism

Turned into rigid lessons

You wave hello

Close your eyes

And before you know it

You've reached you last

'Good-bye'

Minced Words

I was never meant to mince words

But to speak them full

Of vibrancy and flavor

I have tasted and swam through

So many oceans that bring

Little to no sustenance

So much salt burned

My throat and seeped into

Festering wounds

That my tastebuds have been stripped bare

So, what's the use in

Searching for a new love

To savor with senses

That are now rendered useless

Of Shadow and Light

The Constant Fault

Burned from the energy I have

Soaked from the sun

They tell me I am good

With words though

I have none

The older that I grow

The more it is revealed

That the closer I am to death

The deeper I can feel

I am concerto

Mixed of a chaotic

Symphonic opus

Reeling at the chance

For the world to take its notice

Through every painful conflict

And for everything I ever wanted to be

Love was never the cure

But the constant fault in me

Of Shadow and Light

Love Language

My love language is a delicate one

The air thickens with need

It's palpable

I can almost feel your

Heart beating next to me

In the darkness and

Slowly

Without hesitation

Two bodies brush against

one another for the first time

the soft skill of your tongue

caresses my own

take your time with me

I want to learn all of the places

That make you quiver

I am a giver

That is what I will take from this

I only ask for your soul in return

But not until I have slowly

Of Shadow and Light

Lowered my inhibitions

Having yielded to the ache

That sweet and tender ache

And oh, how it throbs

We are two currents

Flowing in perfect synchronization

As the two become one

You wash over me

And I will not stop until

I have heard my name being sung

- And maybe not even then

Of Shadow and Light

Dear Heart

Dear Heart

I'm doing my best to replace you

It's not going so well

I know you had to leave me

Though I don't truly understand just why

Anyway

If you pass on this message

I would be forever grateful

Please tell him that I love him

And that's it's probably best he kept

You for himself

Since I'm not much without

You now anyway

Of Shadow and Light

Vulnerability

I wear vulnerability

Like a second skin

I'm not afraid to show

Where it hurts the most

Because I know that this

Life is short and feel

There is never a point in

Hiding true emotion

Others come and others go

And they take a piece of me with them

And though more often

Then not I allow for this

To happen

I'll still give

I'll still love

Regardless

Of Shadow and Light

Deeply Woven

I fell

So deeply woven into

Your complicated textures

Id almost forgotten who I was

You are a maze

Of never-ending regrets

And lonely hallways

A labyrinth of greatest distortions

Willingly, I took up residence

In your misleading turns

And curves

Never wanting to find my

Way back out of them

I wasn't afraid of being forgotten

If forgotten meant

Being eternally lost

Within you

Of Shadow and Light

Broken Wings

You broke my wings

And then ordered me to fly

You cut my wrists

And then sang to me lullabies

You'd cry out my name

And I would come running

Only to find that I was

The one you'd been hunting

You'd throw me a line

Which would turn into a noose

You'd feed me lie after lie

And I ate up the abuse

Soaked in my shame

Holding hope like a dove

What a simple fool I was

Only to feel what I thought

Was true love

Of Shadow and Light

Adonis

You want to rip out

My sutures

And then help me to heal

You want to cause the attack

And then ask me how it feels

You are the embodiment of Adonis

You swore to never destroy me

Then took back

All you'd promised

You are a sickness from which

I will never recover

The virus that is you

Has convinced me

I will never find another

Of Shadow and Light

Jagged

We were both jagged edges

Of the same blade

Forged by chaos and

Bound by fate

Destined to repeat it all

In a redundant mundane obscurity

Never to realize our deepest

Hopes and dreams

We allowed for them to

Feed our fears

Giving up the best of

Our meager years

What simpleton fools

Were we

Warped by anxieties

Wrapped in trauma

We are the greatest

Of tragedies

Of Shadow and Light

I Miss You

And yet

I still miss you

Even though your words

Could cut me in two

They had a way of healing me

Like no others could

I miss you

Even though your temperature

Fluctuated like flares

From the sun to the

Coldest, deepest and darkest

Recesses of space

When your love shined

Down on me

I was enveloped in a warmth

Comparable to my own

Mother's womb

I still miss you

Even though you never truly

Of Shadow and Light

Wanted me
Even though the love
We shared, to you
Was never true

Of Shadow and Light

Ruined

Ruined

You have ruined every bit of me

Spoiled are the hopes for a future love

You have beat them all

In one fell swoop

You have both set as well

As broken the mold

And have managed to water down

Connections even close to

Any semblance of what we shared

Abandoned is this fragile

Heart of mine

The heart cradled in your bygone

Memory of me

Archaic and tucked away in

Formant cognitions

And still

I live to exist if even only

Within a dream

Of Shadow and Light

2 AM

I wanted someone

To talk to when the insomnia

Kicks in at 2am

Someone to laugh with

Until my stomach hurt so badly

And yet, i still never want

The laughter to end

Someone who cared to take

Notice of my voice when I

Sang alone to some of my

Favorite songs

And especially when I wrote

Some of my own

But life isn't a wishing well

And I've run out of pennies anyway

Of Shadow and Light

3 AM Silence

He fills the 3 AM silence

With warmth and security

Never do I have to wonder

If I am the one he imagines

Lying beside him throughout eternity

We answer one another

Without the need for words

Spoken aloud but with magnetism

Which radiates from our chests

Tethered to one another

We are bound by light

That escapes even the darkest

Of tragedies

Our love envelopes

As well as transcends both

Space and time

Here, I am wanted without

The fear of rejection

With open arms and infinite passion

Of Shadow and Light

Handled with such delicate strength

These ties that bind these

Ties that bind with such divine

Fluidity that one would be fooled

Into believing it was all merely

Just a dream

Of Shadow and Light

Soul Partner

You came into my life
When I had least expected you
You shined a light so bright
I was blinded and consumed
I have been pulled in by
Your gravitational force
Like a massive tidal wave
Crashing onto the shore
You are not the moonbeam
But the sun, bathing me
In a fantastical love anew
Basking in your heat
Your energy
Knowing it was created
Both for me and for you
The heavens conspired
This glorious rendezvous
My love, my soul partner
One soul, split in two

Of Shadow and Light

When You Weren't Looking

When you weren't looking

I crept inside your skin

And made myself comfortable there

I looked around

And lovingly cared for any

Heartbreak that was hiding

Without you aware

I felt

As you began to heal

And made sure that my love would

Last a lifetime

Tending to any broken pieces

That anyone might attribute to

Or who may be unkind

And just so you know

I left behind some of my soul

To always remain within you

So eternally, you might be reminded

Of Shadow and Light

That no matter where you may go

How much you are loved

And that I will never be far

Of Shadow and Light

Grief

Grief is such an unpredictable thing

One day
You're stuck by a stunned silence
That comes from compartmentalizing
Corners you'd forgotten about

The next
You're laughing your head off
Watching old videos of happier times
Times when we were still ignorant

The thoughts that float around
Your mind go from eulogies
To closing the casket on the face
You'd been looking on every day
Since his birth

Of Shadow and Light

You know the initial shock will
Get you through those first
Few days

Then what?

Even now as I sit here
With these tears and thoughts
Thinking about how I will
Ever let them lower you
Into the ground

Of how I'll ever leave you there
Then, walk back to the car and
Into a world without you in it

My sister worries where her daughter is
All the while
I worry about how many
Years that I have left with you

And they'll tell me how
Lucky I am that at least

Of Shadow and Light

You didn't get the worst
Case scenario
I just want to tell them all
To "fuck off" because
That's my little boy
They're talking about

That is the life that I grew
And fought for
The soul that kept me company
On dark and despairing nights
When it was you and I against
The faltering world

As if this disease will have
Any mercy on your frail body
When the time comes
No, they don't realize
The hell that awaits us both

It can happen to any of us
Do you know how many times
I have heard those lines being

Of Shadow and Light

Said to me as if that is going
To make your absence hurt any less

As if I couldn't love every
Bit of you anymore than I
Already do

And that's what I hold
Onto hope for

That my love continues to grow
Like a vine straight up into Heaven
Reaching to you

The tether between you and I, my son

Please climb down
And come for me
When it's my turn
Because I am your mommy
And for you
I will always yearn

Of Shadow and Light

Trauma

I wrap my trauma
With words and all
That I create
I cradle it with love
Patience and compassion
Because beating myself up
For the things that have
Been done to me
Only makes pain thrive longer

Of Shadow and Light

Pressure

Pressure for me means
Having to watch funerals
On a small screen
For little bodies that
Carry the same disease
That he does
Pressure means having
To keep my head held high
While standing on my two feet
Without faltering but it's release
Means hanging around just
A few minutes more
Where pain doesn't exist
And stealing moments
Where I can drop the load
Off at the door of a friend
Or my lover
To help me soothe my soul

Of Shadow and Light

If only

Please just allow me

Just a few seconds more

Of Shadow and Light

Nostalgia

We seek laughter

During street festivals

While holding hands

And singing along to

Tunes from the 90's

We bummed cigarettes

And held the smoke in

I think I can still smell

It's lingering on the wind

Promises kept in pockets

Lined in corduroy

And I still like to line

My combat boots in safety pins

So maybe I'm just trying

To manifest the years, I still

Wasn't aware of how much

Pain was waiting to scuff my soul

That the future meant no

Of Shadow and Light

Longer having your hand to hold

Of Shadow and Light

Deception

I know

I am just a momentary frivolity

Keeping your side of

The monotony warm

Break my shell wide open

Just so you can have a taste

You prefer keeping

Your hands clean

So you use your tongue instead

How the words sound so sweet

They do the job well

You left just enough for me to

Keep them swirling in my mouth

As not to forget the flavor

Of deception coated in sugar

Of Shadow and Light

Dare to Venture

I cannot tell you
Of the souls that I have loved
Of how I have breathed them in
And exhaled them out of me
How my hands have traveled
To places others would
Never dare to venture
And equally so
They have learned this skin
And left marks scarred
Upon it by trekking pathways
Left deeply interwoven within me
So, I dare you to wander
As they have
Since my words will
Only fall short
Of this body and minds
Adventures

Of Shadow and Light

I Am Not in Love

Don't try to tie me down

I am not in love

What a different emotion

To navigate through

I emptied out all

The baggage, though

I am sure I left

Many parts and pieces

Of myself behind where

Love once resided

And yet, I surprisingly

I feel whole

Almost peaceful

And free

Of Shadow and Light

A Letter to My Formal Self

He isn't going to open
Up your mind and read
You like a novel
He isn't going to hear
Your name
Tucked away somewhere
Within his own soul
Like a magically pitched note
Or dream of you in color
In the exact way you
Crave to be seen
He isn't going to
Fall into you
Like a missing puzzle piece
Or recognize you
In some mystical manner
The first time he clasps
Eyes onto you

Of Shadow and Light

Your voice isn't going to
Answer every unanswered
Questions he's ever pondered
To himself because
Life simply does not work
In such enchanting terms
So learn to love it while it lasts
Instead of worrying too much
On the future or living
Any longer within the past
You are only going forward
And there is no way back

Of Shadow and Light

Kaleidoscope

We dared to dream
In kaleidoscope chroma
Meeting in the depths
Of the most alluring escapism
We fought the urge to jump
Time and again
Afraid of the consequences
Petrified of the sin
We touched solace
In momentary embraces
Though never lasting long
As our intertwined
Fantasies lost their validity
We set fuel to the fire
And watched as our beloved
Illusion of enchantment
Burned to a cinder

Of Shadow and Light

Consequential Love

If life didn't come
With consequences
You wouldn't be sitting
Where you are
With your conscience in
Your hands
You would've broken the skin
Right down clear to the bone
If it meant ripping their truth
From out of them
Did they really love you
Were their intentions pure
Were all those long
And lonely nights
Spent laying on a
Salt-soaked pillow
Worth the pain
The same pillow you once

Of Shadow and Light

Laid your love drunken head upon

In those moments they

Promised you forever

Or would you throw all

Of those principles

Right out the door

Just for a taste

Of sweet revenge

On your tongue

Of Shadow and Light

Autumnal Grief

My hearts grief

Sings a solemn song

With the first fallen

Leaf of autumn

I drew breath for

The first time

In the spring when love

Blossomed into the

Thing of dreams

Though anytime fall

Came near

I choked on the cruelest

Of fears

Only to be drowned in

It's dreadful premonition

Oh, how I long to sink

Into the spring just once more

Of Shadow and Light

Hourglass Love

If you could only see

The beauty held

For you within these veins

Then maybe the

Love for what I once

Carried for you

Could withstands the

Way you tore at it

But as sand passes through

The hourglass

So shall the collection

Of our love and all

Words passed between

Us with it

Of Shadow and Light

Lonely Souls

Is this the place

Where all the

Lonely souls go

Do we dig our own graves

And go out quietly

Or do we kick and scream

Because this wasn't the

Way things were supposed

To go

Our ending wasn't meant

To come to a closure

With solely me

Without you

Of Shadow and Light

The Void

Cracked and splintered

I fall into the void

Your words have

Gathered at my feet

And left me

Here to drown

Aimless and gutted

No one can hear

My screams

My voice is lost

To the darkness

Of the ethers

A hollowed cavity

That was once our dream

Of Shadow and Light

Bled

Bled
From the chapters
Of my unbound book
Tasted from each curve
Of my exposed spine
I let him drink from every
Open and willing source
Of love that flowed from me
To which he found
That I was a well of
Replenishment he never
Realized he always needed
From my heart
To my soul
To my mouth and below
As we exchanged every
Passionate glance
To the rhythm of melodious
And heartfelt notes

Of Shadow and Light

Conceal

How do we conceal

Scars that still ache

Where do we find

The pieces lost

Once our hearts finally break

How do we vanquish

The constant resounding fears

How do we recover love

That was shed

In flowing tears

Of Shadow and Light

Sliced Open

You sliced me open
From hope to despair
Without a care for what
It would do to me
You fed from my wounds
After ripping me apart
And then told me
How I shouldn't have
Played with knives

Of Shadow and Light

Bitter

I am bitter

Aggrieved

And discontented

I am filled with

Disdain and resentment

I was lead to believe

A great love waited me

Then he took what he

Needed and then left it

Of Shadow and Light

Rainy Day Playlist

I was never sculpted
Into your words
Or your rainy-day playlist
I was lucky if I was ever
The dust that built up
Along your baseboards
I cherished the times
When I was a place
You would lay your
Lonely head upon
When time was heavy
In your faltering hands
And now I think I mourn
What could have been
If such little adoration
Could grow from just
These few seeds we shared
That were never sewn

Of Shadow and Light

Eternal Balance

Felling heavy

I am tipsy and unsteady

Longing for eternal balance

I've sprinkled grains

Of sand to the wind

Tied to hopeful whispers

Praying for angels to

Hear my plea

That I am begging

For forgiveness

Maybe it takes a

Collective amount of

Penance to receive an

Absolution in order

For these prayers to be

Answered

Of Shadow and Light

Twenty-Eight Stitches

It was the summer of
Nineteen eighty-seven
When I tip-toed to the
Guest bath as to not get
Caught with cat litter on
The soles of my feet
It was also the same day
I was rushed to the hospital
To have twenty-eight stitches
In my forehead
That was the first time
I understood how cartoon
Characters always saw stars
When they were hit on the head
I remember my dad lifting me up
So that I could glance
Into the hospital mirror to check
The damage out for myself
As well as the needle injected

Of Shadow and Light

Into my forehead by the
Plastic surgeon when I laid
Still on the emergency room stretcher
I'll be damned if I didn't
Shed one tear either

Of Shadow and Light

Misplaced Fortunes

What did we do

With these misplaced fortunes

We've thrown each chance

Of hope not cautiously

To the wind

But tied them down

And locked them up

With furrowed brows

Heaviness lays sprawled

Upon our optimism

We have cast away

Every word

Every promise we'd

Ever made to one another

As if we had found the

Fountain of youth

Somewhere hidden

As if tomorrow was

Of Shadow and Light

Never coming

Of Shadow and Light

Sometimes

Sometimes it's too late to
Cover up the tracks
That are left behind
By neglect that are
Buried deeply
Within the quagmires
Of time less spent
Sometimes it's too late
To dig up from the
Quicksand of love lost
Love that's been for granted
At a measurable cost
And sometimes its better
To take the seeds of what
We have leftover and to
Plant them to leave
Blooming buds free to grow
And use the vine

Of Shadow and Light

As a lesson

Oh, if only

Sometimes

Of Shadow and Light

Beyond Measure

If I had to create anything

Close to your resemblance

I would have to piece together

One by one the souls

Of many and still

It could not amount

To the needs that you

Have met beyond measure

Of Shadow and Light

Absolution

I found absolution

To be a potent cure

For the soul

Not only in letting go

Of what others have done

But in releasing the harmful

Things that I've said to myself

I forgive me for speaking

Down to the girl who was

Just trying to find love

In ways that would often

Come back to haunt her

And now I am clothed

In grace and it makes

For the most beautiful garments

Of Shadow and Light

Carnal Desires

Delicious instruments
Of such carnal desires
We tasted
We fell
We jumped headfirst
Into the pyre
I am Aphrodite in love
I am the sweetest of wines
As moans escape my lips
And you sip between my thighs
Hand over all your pain
I promise
I will conquer
Soothe and take away
I was meant to be your lover
In this intoxicating rapture
I am boundless
I'll set us free
As I glide slowly onto you

Of Shadow and Light

And you release into me

Of Shadow and Light

Storm

When did this storm begin?
The one between you and me
I am a man thrown
Overboard thrashed violently
Upon your troubled sea
A kaleidoscope of muddied
Watercolors on your canvas
Of concocted distress
Where lies of tumultuous variations
Sound off a distorted prejudice
I've never known a soul
Quite so masterful
You have it down to an art
Split wide your chest
Truth reveals to me
How unsurprisingly

- You have no heart

Of Shadow and Light

Lighter Fluid

I doused my mind
With lighter fluid
In hopes of burning you
From all memory
But tears rained down
Flooding every crevice
Pooling into puddles
Thus, rotting sutures
Allowing for infection
To fester in places that I had
Forgotten about
All the gentle
Moments which once
Transpired between us
Leaving behind
New wounds left agape
For me to tend to

Of Shadow and Light

Sweater

Falling out of love

Is almost just as sad

As a broken heart

Sort of like when you

Lose your favorite sweater

Or when you realize

You no longer fancy

That pasta dish you

Always ordered from

The Italian restaurant in town

We frequented often

It's like listening to

Your favorite song

And it just doesn't hit

The same way anymore

It leaves you questioning

'Now what do I do?'

I guess I could always

Just go out and buy

Of Shadow and Light

A new sweater

Of Shadow and Light

Dove

You broke my wings

And then ordered me to fly

You cut my wrists

And then sang to me lullabies

You'd cry out my name

And I would come running

Only to find that I

Was the one you'd

Been hunting

You'd throw me a line

Which would turn

Into a noose

You'd feed me lie after lie

And I ate up the abuse

Soaked in my shame

Holding hope like a dove

What a simple fool

I was only to feel what

I thought was

Of Shadow and Light

True love

Of Shadow and Light

Genius of Art

We are a broken promise

A genius of art

A painting ruined

In the rain

We were the anticipation

Of love

Only to be turned down

Once again

You were poison

Coated in a thick

Sugar glaze

You are the last breath

Greedily takes

You are a wound packed in salt

A paper cut drenched

In lemon

We are a shattered porcelain vase

And I am the one left

Of Shadow and Light

To suffer

Picking up all the pieces

You've left abandoned

Of Shadow and Light

Mirage

If only
If only I could rip you
From the innermost dwellings
Of my impressionable mind
These dopamine receptors
Have branded all memory of you
Fooling me into believing
Subconsciously you loved
Me too
You are fool's gold
A treasure bearing no worth
An investment without gain
You are a mirage
And I ran headfirst into you
Hoping to quench my thirst
With parched lips and
A calloused heart
Only to lose the race
And end up back at the start

Of Shadow and Light

Waves

You are the sound of

The waves

Crashing onto the shore

You are the relief of a breeze

When the sun beams too warm

You are that first sip of water

To quench my aching thirst

You are the storybook romance

That keeps me immersed

You are my courage

When I have given up

And the comfort to my malaise

You are the reason

That I carry on

The only soul that I crave

And when all else fails me

In which I know this life

Is through

I'd rather no other

Of Shadow and Light

To lay beside me, my love

Than you

Of Shadow and Light

Your Name

You

You are a shell

Of such tragic beauty

Though your mind is

A conundrum

Of self-inflicted wounds

It was your spark

Your fire

The burn drew me in

Even though it burned

And now these scars

Are all that I have left

To remind me that you

Were once a part of the

Force that kept this heart

Beating

And mercilessly

It keeps pounding and pounding

And in the constant thrust

Of Shadow and Light

Of each relentless pump

I can still hear your name

Repeating

Of Shadow and Light

My Murderer

I am locked

Set in place

Frozen within the confines

Of what was meant to be

Of where he left me

In bitter and vile rejection

Bleeding from the depths

Of a wound

Only fulfilled with

Distraction

Forced to forget

To push away

To rip from this skin

And he had left laced

And imprinted within it

And yet

I still long for -

I still love my murderer

Of Shadow and Light

Destroy Me

Seduce me

With your words

And your song

Heal me

Help me right

All my wrongs

Crash into me

The way the moon

Pulls the tides

To the shore

Destroy me

To the point

Where I am begging

For only you

Evermore

Of Shadow and Light

Lock and Key

Mind is scattered

Lovers yearning

He's the fire

And I am burning

For far too long

Quench this thirst

For I fear my heart

May burst

Heat is rising

From off my skin

I am quivering

With need for him

I'm the lock

And he's the key

Oh, how he belongs

Deep inside of me

Of Shadow and Light

Shell

When you fall away from me

I fade

I become a shell

Of my former self

The she that I am with you

You ebb and flow

In and out of my life

But when you flow back in

The blood rushes and returns

As does the color of

My heart and skin

And I hold onto what

Precious words we exchange once again

As well as the incomparable

Love that we share

Proving to me true

That I need you

As I need air to breathe

Of Shadow and Light

Lighthouse

I am a lighthouse

A beacon for all to see

Worn down by emptiness

Battered by grief

My lamp light

Guides the broken

Even when I am dim

Downtrodden by exhaust

Hollowed out from within

Still, I am a lighthouse

Aglow for all to see

But once I cease to shine

Will you remember me

Of Shadow and Light

Confessors

I've traded this old skin

For something clean

Stripping these stitches

Of damp antiquity

That left the scars and sins

Of pleasure skewed

Reviving myself like a

Cathartic act of penance

As these words drip

From my sullen fingers

Onto the pages

These are the pages of

My life's story

These pages are my confessors

Of Shadow and Light

Dwell

I dwelled within you

In those moments

When breath quickened and lips

Suffocated all reason

Every part of you

Explored every inch of me

And led to a thirst

Aching from your

Parched lips

And how I quenched

The drought you had

Succumbed to

A new depth was explored

In distances we never

Imagined were within reach

Looking from behind

Or hovering just above

We gathered up our strength

And climbed peaks of euphoria

Of Shadow and Light

We conquered the pain

With a gentle thrust

Into inevitable ecstasy

Of Shadow and Light

Beckoning

I'm not quite sure

How to put the words together

In my mind

But it is you and I

And this new

But ancient love we have

Created between us

We are locked eyes

Speaking languages

Others could never understand

You have existed underneath

This skin for a millennia

We are a fluidity

A constant humming

And now I finally understand

What that small echo within me

Was whispering

It was you all along

Of Shadow and Light

Beckoning my spirit

To return to yours

Of Shadow and Light

Filter

I cannot say why

You carried me under false

Pretenses

I found my place in

This beautiful lie

And I willingly played pretend

You spoke of forever

And our eternity

Of the stars

The moon and the sky

Until one day you

You grew cold

And left me to find

Another path

As time went on

A new love grew

However, not the same

A love so careful

Of Shadow and Light

A love that's safe

A mere filter to ease the pain

Tell me, my love

What choice was given to me

This was the best

That I could do

So I will give him

What warmth I have left

The love that was meant

For you

Of Shadow and Light

Vibrancy

Break me from

This cold void

Of expectations

I need to see the

Vibrancy of color again

To feel freedom

In the wind

To grasp ahold

To passions that

Tear our yearnings

From the outside in

Teach me what it

Feels like to release

This trapped soul of mine

So deeply lost within

Of Shadow and Light

Absolution

I found absolution

To be a potent cure

For the soul

Not only in letting go

Of what others have done

But in releasing

The harmful things I've said

To myself

I forgive me

For talking down to

The girl who was just

Trying to find love

In the ways that would

Often come back to haunt her

And now, I am clothed in grace

And it makes for the

Most beautiful garments

Of Shadow and Light

Mirror

Seeing myself

Once the mirror is no

Longer fogged

I am steadied by a broken hand

Which you stood upon

Gurgling drips from stitches

Bleeding but numb

Thirsty for your words

Though I receive none

Grasping at straws

But I choke on them instead

Awake but fast asleep

You, the perpetual ghost

Living inside of my head

Of Shadow and Light

Sunsets

Love isn't formed on

Sunsets alone

It's trauma bonds and

Similar pain

It's toxic

Unrequited and often

Given in vain

Love can be a beggar

A swollen

Heavy heart

The thing that glues us together

Or the pain that rips us apart

Of Shadow and Light

Moment's Notice

Sometimes

And without moment's notice

It surfaces abruptly

Like a slap to the face

Or a blast of frigid air

Causing my bones to shake

My lips to quiver

Eyes to swell with salt

It is the hollowness

The reminder

That where love once lived

Flourished and breathed

It's warmth into me

I am now merely a solitary vessel

On my own

Of Shadow and Light

The New

Life will never return
To the way it once was
I can never reverse what has happened
To our lives
Ta happier
More carefree existence
When we still had the world in our
Ever eager
Optimistic hands
I cannot bring the little souls back
To life that have gone before me
I cannot take away the monster
That ages my son so quickly
I cannot rip his body of its DNA
For repairs
I cannot make time stand still
Though, I can burn the
Present into my mind
I can hope for a little more time

Of Shadow and Light

And I can at least
Pray that when the time
Does come to say good-bye
That I will follow him closely behind
These are the realities and consequences
Of bringing life into the world

Of Shadow and Light

Paper Thin Skin

We created such beautiful

Magic out of these broken fragments

That even the softest of notes

Carry the sweetest of melodies

We've etched together

These pieces one by one

From off the juices of our

Delicate tongues

As passion claws its way

Out from underneath our

Paper thin skin

Tethering our rhyme

As together we unite in our sins

Of Shadow and Light

Home

Home feels like
The smell of patchouli
Filling my lungs
Petrichor and wet wood
Crows cawing outside my window
On an early autumn morning
Or late winters eve
Snowfall soon follows
A fire that burns in my
Heart and in my home
And a bottle of vino rosso
Smoke filling the air when
I opened my door
And memories of falling
Asleep in your arms
So that when I look back
Home isn't quite so far

Of Shadow and Light

Reasons

I wonder if we all
Write for the same
Reasons, as if these
Poems are in some
Way meant to be
A magical spell
Hoping our hearts
Desire will come true
By putting pen to paper
And throwing them
Out into the universe

Of Shadow and Light

Death

We view death

From an outside

Point of view

We are here though

Separate but remain

Tethered

Energy is constant

It does not end

It's power transfers

Even if we cannot see with

The naked eye

We perceive this truth

Through a blinding veil

Just as The Almighty

Immovable Mover

Lays His gentle hand

Upon our pain

Death comes to us all

Of Shadow and Light

Strive to fight the good fight

To love without boundaries

As we do not die in vain

Of Shadow and Light

Spectacle

You are a spectacle -
A means of entertainment
For the masses
You're bleeding
Profusely in front of
Them all and no one
Stops to cauterize the flow
Instead, they lap up every
Last drop with false
Sympathies and elation
On their faces
This was the plan all along
You were the slaughter
For the sacrifice

Of Shadow and Light

Wash, Rinse and Repeat

I always say
How I feel like a rung out
Washcloth
Once the day is over
I wash, rinse and repeat
For another inevitable
Ride on this emotional
Roller coaster we call life
I feel soaked in grief
For things that haven't
Even come to be
And for things that already have
Maybe I should add some
Fabric softener
To the next load

Of Shadow and Light

The Taste of Love

Love tastes like salt

Stained on your neck

At the tip of my tongue

After you've had your

Way with me

Love indulges in the

Middle of the night

When the warmth

Of your mouth

Nestles between my legs

Love sounds a lot like

The melody of

A crescendo climax and

Moans that cannot

Be contained

Love feels and is perpetual

When our bodies search

For peace

And find home in

Of Shadow and Light

The arms of one another

At the end of the day

Of Shadow and Light

Starter Fluid

I doused my mind

With starter fluid

In hopes of burning you

From all memory

But tears rained

Down, flooding every

Crevasse

Pooling into

Puddles, thus rotting sutures

Allowing for infection to

Fester in places that I had

Forgotten about

All the gentle

Moments which once

Transpired between

Us, leaving behind

New wounds left agape

For me to tend to

Of Shadow and Light

Love Should Never Be

I miss you
As the frost covered ground misses
The warmth of the summer sun
I miss you
For all the words left unsaid
For all the things left undone
I need you
As the human form requires a soul
To essentially exist
I love you
But love should never have to feel
As desperate, as wanting
As this

Of Shadow and Light

Lemonade

Sometimes love comes softly

And then it comes hard

There is no point in

Comparing apples to oranges

You make the lemonade

And forget to add the sugar

We pile up our false prophets

Leaving us left with little

To believe in

And yet we just keep

On hoping

That kissing frogs leads

To princes and fairytale

Endings

Of Shadow and Light

Shoreline

There isn't as much
Fear of the water
When you are one
Foot in and one out
Testing the temperature
And praying it is warmer
Than tepid comfort
While waiting for the current
To subside just ankle deep
Though the desire to
Know what exists
Just beyond the reef
Watching, waiting
Withholding from
The venture
And ultimately settling
For the security
Of the shoreline instead

Of Shadow and Light

Micros

*Just because you can't see
the light doesn't mean it isn't
shining somewhere.*
TMC

Of Shadow and Light

Belonging

She felt him

On her skin

Before he'd even

Touched her

She belonged to him

In that way

And no one else

Could quite

Compare

Of Shadow and Light

Recognize

Hold me

Let me heal

Within the stillness

Of your arms

There is a brokenness

I recognize in you

That resides within me too

Of Shadow and Light

Meaning

I didn't know
My name carried so
Much meaning until
I heard it whispered
By you

Of Shadow and Light

Drug

And like the drug you are
You get me high
But nothing lasts forever

Of Shadow and Light

Within My Dreams

If within my dreams
Is the only place
Where I can find you
Never wake me from
My blissful slumber

Of Shadow and Light

Madness

If loving you is madness
I willingly relinquish all sanity

Of Shadow and Light

Courage

They fear her courage
And that is where her
Strength over them lies

Of Shadow and Light

Soul

There wasn't a soul quite
As deep as the one
She carried around in her
And maybe that's how
He so easily got lost within it

Of Shadow and Light

My Heart

I don't know
How to give
Any more than I
Already have
So if you've
Finished with
My heart please
Kindly hand it back

Of Shadow and Light

Cruel

What is life

But the cruel ache

For something that is missing

And can never be found

Of Shadow and Light

Tangled

I am a tangled

Up mess

Of a woman

But wouldn't you

Still love to try

And unravel me

Of Shadow and Light

Forged

I do believe

That this heart of mine

To be carefully forged

With you in mind

Of Shadow and Light

Tragedy

No one wants

To read the happy ending

We're all broken

Give us the tragedy

Of Shadow and Light

Mountain

She was more

Than just the mountain

Standing before them

She was the river that

Raged right through

Of Shadow and Light

Tripping

I knew it too much
This love that I carried
I should've never left it
Lying it at your feet
It was never my intention
To have you tripping over me

Of Shadow and Light

Wounds

It's okay

Go ahead and place the blame

Into my clean hands

Twist my words

Sprinkle a little salt on top

And then

Rub those self-inflicted wounds

Of yours with them

Of Shadow and Light

Moonlight

Let me bathe in
Your moonlight
Smother me in
Midnight kisses
Make love to me
In the twilight
Envelop me in your
Warmth and starlit
Darkness

Of Shadow and Light

Bitterness Wept

Bitterness wept

When the sweetness

Of your lips met mine

Of Shadow and Light

In Helping You

In helping you
Find your way
I eventually lost myself

Of Shadow and Light

Sun and Moon

Like the sun

You will gravitate toward her

And like the moon

You'll be locked in place

Of Shadow and Light

Beautiful Way

She had a beautiful way
Of turning pain
Into love for others

Of Shadow and Light

Laced Deceit

How beautifully
You've laced your deceit
As you siphoned the love
From out of me

Of Shadow and Light

Character

What you have done
To me shows your character
How I loved you regardless
Shows mine

Of Shadow and Light

Life Preserver

She was the life preserver

Pulling them from

Treacherous waves

For others she was

The sea itself

They'd drown within

Of Shadow and Light

Artificial Sweetener

If true love is the purest of sugars

I'm pretty you were just

An artificial sweetener

Of Shadow and Light

Acceptance

I am learning acceptance
That I was never too much
You just couldn't handle
All that I am made of

Of Shadow and Light

Tragically

Are we fantastic in pretending
To be in love
Or are we tragically breaking
Our own hearts

Of Shadow and Light

Giver

I was always too much
Of a giver until there
Was only so much in
Which I could take

Of Shadow and Light

Truth

The truth is
I fell in love
And I may never
Recover

Of Shadow and Light

Answers

When I look to my
Heart for answers
Your face is all I can see

Of Shadow and Light

Stuff of Stars

If you and I

Are made from

The same stuff

Of the stars

It's no wonder

I should gravitate

That I should orbit

Nearest you

Of Shadow and Light

Yours

Of all the things

I've ever wanted to be

Being yours

Was top of

My list

Of Shadow and Light

Sanguine Veil

My love fell

Hidden between a glass

Blade and a sanguine veil

It bled dry to the memory

Of hope that yours

Would one day be the

Reflection staring back

At me

Of Shadow and Light

Tip of Your Tongue

My name belongs

At the tip of your

Tongue

Like a spell that

Cannot be broken

Of Shadow and Light

Cuts Deeply

Don't be surprised
If what I say cuts deeply
When you're the one
Who handed me the knife

Of Shadow and Light

Loved By a Poet

To be loved by a poet
Is to find love hidden
Secretly in between
The lines of so many things

Of Shadow and Light

Control

I can't control
The things my heart
Desires any more than
You can control
That I am not
What you do

Of Shadow and Light

Power

Try as you may
You can't destroy
Someone with that
Much power in her love

Of Shadow and Light

Explain

How do I explain to
The arms that knew you well
To hold onto myself instead

Of Shadow and Light

Heal

You should never break
Apart from loving someone
Love is meant to heal
Not destroy us

Of Shadow and Light

Whole

Tell me if in
In breaking me apart
You now feel whole
Again

Of Shadow and Light

New Year

Another new year
But the same old me
Still trying to carry on
Without you

Of Shadow and Light

Hard

I didn't mean to love you
But you've made it so
Hard not to

Of Shadow and Light

Expands

I want a love

That expands like the universe

And then collapses and envelops me

Give me a love that saturates my being

Of Shadow and Light

Spell

My name belongs

At the tip of your

Tongue

Like a spell that

Cannot be broken

Of Shadow and Light

Poetry

The more I learn
I have found poetry
To be less about love
And more about survival

Of Shadow and Light

Aim

If it is ever your
Aim to hurt me
Don't worry
I break my own
Heart with its
Expectations

Of Shadow and Light

Deaf Ears

And I hope that my voice
Is the last thing you remember
When all your desperate pleas
Fall on deaf ears

Of Shadow and Light

Seeps

Lose yourself in me
The way the rain
Seeps into the sea

Of Shadow and Light

Quietly

I knew you would
Quietly find happiness
In places where I do
Not exist

Of Shadow and Light

Hell

You were once an
Escape from the
Hells that I faced
And now you're
Just another one
Added into the fold

Of Shadow and Light

The Fire

She has lived hells

Most men would cower from

And still walks out of

The fire with her

Head held high

Of Shadow and Light

Crumble

I build things up
In my mind to be
Something they're not
And then wonder why
It hurts so much
When I eventually
Crumble

Of Shadow and Light

Buy

All hearts should come with

A "You break it, you buy it" policy

If you play with someone's

Affections

Expect for there

To be consequences

Of Shadow and Light

In My Silence

I didn't want someone
To save me
Just someone who
Understood me
Even in my silence

Of Shadow and Light

Monotony

I lost myself
In the monotony of the
Person that you wanted
Me to be
And now I am
Struggling to find
The person that I was
Meant to

Of Shadow and Light

Heard

I am a woman
With words and verse
Among these curses
And I will fight until
The bitter end for
Every bit of them to
Be heard

Of Shadow and Light

I Am Not the Moon

I'm not going

Through a phase

My dear

I am not the moon

And you are not

A definition that

I must adhere to

Of Shadow and Light

Shines

Oh, but how she shines

In the most glorious of lights

And isn't she worth

Every bit of its burn

Of Shadow and Light

Acceptance

The scars of rejection
Take longer to fade
Than the healing of
Acceptance and I
Am still trying to
Navigate that journey

Of Shadow and Light

Mask

The mask you're
Wearing is cracking
And the truth is
Leaking through

Of Shadow and Light

Webs

I often get caught
In webs of nostalgia
Wondering which one
Of us was the
Spider or the fly

Of Shadow and Light

Taste

What a beautiful taste
You left in my mouth
The last time you had
Me pinned up against
The wall

Of Shadow and Light

Her Heart

Her heart is a home

Give it comfort and love

And she will provide

You shelter

Of Shadow and Light

Worth

Tell me what it takes
To earn your love
Because if there's
Anything worth working for
It's you

Of Shadow and Light

Ravish

Ravish me
Turn me into
Moving poetry

Of Shadow and Light

Unrealized Dream

You were only ever
Just a dream that
Would never be
Realized

Of Shadow and Light

Astray

My heart is exhausted
From chasing
Others down paths that
Always lead me astray

Of Shadow and Light

Embers

Dropped like breadcrumbs
Were the flames
Of your desires
And now I'm living
Off embers
While your someone else's fire

Of Shadow and Light

Dwindles

Don't blame me for
How love dwindles down
To a simmer
When you are no where
To be found

Of Shadow and Light

Conundrum

I feel too much
In an unfeeling world
And therein lies the
Conundrum that is me

Of Shadow and Light

Learning

I may be broken
And I am hurting
But above all
I am learning

Of Shadow and Light

Stumble

You don't walk away
From me you stumble
Tripping over excuses
Being led by lies

Of Shadow and Light

Unlearn

Having to unlearn
Loving you has
To be one of the hardest
Things I've ever had to do

Of Shadow and Light

Ache

And when I look back
To all the things
That made me ache
It's always you -
I only see your face

Of Shadow and Light

Junkie

If love is an addiction
Then I am its junkie

Of Shadow and Light

You Don't Love Me

Don't be afraid
To tell me you don't
Love me
I've heard those
Words before

Of Shadow and Light

True

When it's true and real
You won't have to chase
Or fight for it to want you

Of Shadow and Light

Convey

And you will find
There is much truth
Within these hands
As I convey it all
Onto the page

Of Shadow and Light

Chasing

I kept running away
From what healed me
Because I was constantly
Chasing after you

Of Shadow and Light

How Many Lies

I wonder

How many lies it took

For them to realize

Your truth

Of Shadow and Light

Memory

Let her be the masterpiece

At the tip of your fingers

Paint every curve

Until you know her by memory

Of Shadow and Light

You and Me

Because if it isn't you and me

Then I don't want it

Of Shadow and Light

Unwrap

Unwrap my calloused
Heart
I promise I am softer
Just under the surface

Of Shadow and Light

Option

How many times
Will it take before
The truth finally
Gets through to me
That I was only
Ever an option to you
And never a priority

Of Shadow and Light

Excuses

Please don't waste my time
With feeding me honey dipped words
Only to leave me swallowed whole
In a sticky mess of your excuses

Of Shadow and Light

Drowning

I knew you were the ocean
When I dove in headfirst
But I had to take the chance
Even if it meant drowning
In you

Of Shadow and Light

Outline

I can barely remember
A time when pain didn't
Outline every action of mine

Of Shadow and Light

Silence

Some days I don't speak
But my silence
Screams in volumes

Of Shadow and Light

As I Am

Take me as I am

Consume me

Love me

Or leave me

The hell alone

Of Shadow and Light

Absence

Now what else is there we share

Other than the absence

Of one another

Of Shadow and Light

Kingdom

So many pillars of my

Life have fallen

Now I stand a kingdom

On its own

You can find more of TMC's work by following her on social media:

Instagram: @TMCPoetry
Twitter: @PoetryTMC
TikTok: @tmcpoetrywritings
Facebook: @TMCPoetryQuotes
Pinterest: @tmcpoetry

Her first poetry collection
'The Remnants of Love Lost'
is also available on Amazon.com, as well as all other major online bookstores.

Of Shadow and Light

About the author:

We'll call her "T". Born in Tampa, Florida the summer of 1981 and now residing in Georgia, she has always been in the artistic scope in life and cleaves to her art in many fashions; a poet, a novelist, a writer, a photographer, a musician, and a singer-songwriter. She is the mother of five children, the eldest now eighteen the victim of Cockayne Syndrome, a non-curable, life shortening disease. And a result, it has become her passion to help others, reaching out as she is called. Please take these words and apply them to soothe that which may be hurting.
Yours in Christ …

Of Shadow and Light

Made in the USA
Middletown, DE
19 March 2022